Heiwa

Maluna aʻe o nā lāhui apau ke ola ke kanaka
"Above all nations is humanity"

The Spark M. Matsunaga Institute for Peace of the University of Hawaiʻi is an academic community designed to develop and share knowledge about the root causes of violence, the conditions of peace, and the use of nonviolent means for resolving conflicts. Founded in 1985, the institute operates with openness to all views and with a commitment to academic freedom and rigor. It is committed to improving education in peace studies for graduate, undergraduate, secondary, and primary school students; undertaking peace research to promote understanding of issues of violence, nonviolence, social justice, ecological vitality, freedom, and human dignity; participating with community groups to communicate with all segments of society on these issues; and publishing scholarly and creative works on peace in all media.

Peace Poetry in

English and Japanese

EDITED BY

Jiro Nakano and Brien Hallett

Spark M. Matsunaga Institute for Peace
University of Hawai'i ■ Honolulu, Hawai'i

© 1995 Spark M. Matsunaga Institute for Peace
All rights reserved
Printed in the United States of America

Library of Congress Cataloging-in-Publication Data
HEIWA (peace) : peace poetry in English and Japanese /
edited by Jiro Nakano and Brien Hallett.
p. cm.
ISBN 0–8248–1813–X
1. Japanese poetry—20th century—Translations into English. 2. Waka—Translations into
English. 3. Haiku—Translations into English. 4. American poetry—20th century—
Translations into Japanese. 5. English poetry—20th century—Translations into Japanese.
6. Peace—Poetry. 7. Matsunaga, Spark M., 1916– .
I. Nakano, Jiro. II. Hallett. Brien.
PL782.E3H45 1996
895.6'104—dc20   95-42220
                                                          CIP

This book is printed on acid-free paper and meets the guideline for
permanence and durability of the Council on Library Resources.

Manufacture of this book was through the production services
program of the University of Hawai'i Press

Text calligraphy by Kasuaki Tanahashi

Distributed by
University of Hawai'i Press
Order Department
2840 Kolowalu Street
Honolulu, Hawai'i 96822

Senator Spark Masuyaki Matsunaga

1916-1990

Peacemaker

Mortals' Tool

Last night again I dreamed of you,
    As nightly oft I do;
I dreamed of scenes as child I'd seen,
    Of castle heights and world serene.

Nocturnal sleep, as gift to man,
    On hopeful pictures lifts all bars,
The words to sting awakening youth,
    As growing light uncovers truth.

'Twas not for man to kill a man;
    'Twas meant for man to love a man;
Yet who am I but mortals' tool,
    No better than a monarch's fool,
To play a part on earth assigned,
    No choice, no will, afraid, resigned.

Lieutenant Spark Matsunaga
Italy, November 16, 1943

人間達の用具

昨夜また貴方の夢を見た、
毎夜しばしば見るように。
それは、子供の頃夢見た，城塞のある
静かな世界の風景のようだった。

夜の眠りは、人への賜のように、
希望をもたらし、全ての障害を持ち上げる。
光が広がって真実を照らし出すように、
その言葉は目覚める若者を苦しめる。

人間は、人を殺めるためにではなく、
人を愛するために生きるべきなのだが、
私は人間達のただの用具では無かったか。
私はただ王者の道化師でしかない。
選ばず、意志もなく、恐れ諦めて、
命令されるままこの世に遊び戯れるのだ。

1943年11月16日、
イタリア戦線にて
スパーキー. マツナガ

CONTENTS

ACKNOWLEDGMENTS

A special thank you to

Shoyei Hatta
for the cover calligraphy

Kazuaki Tanahashi
for the text calligraphy

Jiro Nakano and Joseph Stanton
for translating the Japanese
poems into English

Jiro Nakano and Tatsuo Teraoka
for translating the English
poems into Japanese

PREFACE

Heiwa: Peace Poetry in Japanese and English is the result of a need meeting an opportunity. Since its inception in 1986, the Institute for Peace has been looking for a way to honor the late United States Senator from Hawai'i, Spark Matsunaga. As a student at the University of Hawai'i in 1941, with the clouds of war darkening the horizon, Spark Matsunaga dreamed of establishing a United States Academy of Peace to stimulate knowledge of and interest in peace. In 1984, after much hard work and effort, his dream came to fruition. The United States Institute of Peace was established in Washington, D.C., following the passage of legislation that Senator Matsunaga had sponsored. Shortly after his death in 1990, the University of Hawai'i changed the name of the University of Hawai'i Institute for Peace to the Spark M. Matsunaga Institute for Peace. While this dedication of the Institute to the ideals and vision of Senator Matsunaga certainly expressed our respect and regard, many at the Institute felt that something more tangible was needed.

The opportunity came in March of 1992 when I brought a remarkable anthology of tanka to the attention of the Institute's Publications Committee. The book, *Poets Behind Barbed Wire,*[*] is exceptional not just for the quality of its poetry, but even more so for the circumstances under which it was written. The title refers not to the sharp and pointed character of the poems, but to the very real barbed wire that encircled the internment camps in which the poets were imprisoned during World War II. Living in tar-paper barracks, these Japanese-Americans documented the sad irony of their imprisonment in the poignant and direct manner that only poetry can achieve.

After reading *Poets Behind Barbed Wire,* the other members of the Publications Committee concurred with my suggestion that a bilingual Japanese-English volume of peace poetry dedicated to Senator Matsunaga would be a most fitting and tangible tribute. The committee, which was then composed of Tom Brislin, Department of Journalism, John Haak, University Librarian, Richard Joun, Hawai'i Department of Business Education

---

[*]Keiho Soga, Taisanboku Mori, Sojin Takei, and Munin Ozaki, *Poets Behind Barbed Wire,* ed. and trans. Jiro Nakano and Kay Nakano (Honolulu: Bamboo Ridge Press, 1983).

Development and Tourism, George Simson, Center for Biographical Research, Mary Tiles, Department of Philosophy, and myself, was particularly enthusiastic because it believed that the arts, in general, and poetry, in particular, promote peace in a powerful and positive manner. By bringing together poets from different cultures, the contest itself would contribute to and enhance our mutual search for peace and understanding in this tormented world. In addition, the members of the committee were struck by how well the combination of poetry and peace epitomized Senator Matsunaga's life and work. For, not only was the Senator a tireless worker for peace, but also he frequently turned to poetry throughout his life whenever he reflected upon the mysteries of the human dilemma, as the Senator's poem printed on the dedication page illustrates.

To get the project moving, I contacted the man who had provided the original inspiration, Dr. Jiro Nakano, the editor and translator of *Poets Behind Barbed Wire*. Dr. Nakano, a physician and poet living in Hilo and member of the Ginu-shisha Tanka Club, graciously consented to meet with the Publications Committee when next he flew to Honolulu. He also suggested that Frances Kakugawa and Darold Braida, two poets and educators in Honolulu well versed in these matters, join us so that we could avail ourselves of their knowledge and experience. When I phoned them, both enthusiastically agreed to attend our meeting and assist us in the project. At the meeting, all agreed that a bilingual volume of poetry would be an appropriate way to honor Senator Matsunaga. It was further agreed that the Institute should sponsor a poetry contest centered on the theme of peace and that both haiku and tanka would be accepted in both Japanese and English. Stanley Schab, then the editor at the Institute for Peace, immediately set to work organizing the contest, which was held during the fall of 1992.

One hundred and seventy-seven poets from Japan, Hawai'i, the mainland United States, Canada, Brazil, and England submitted over eight hundred poems, from which our judges made the final selection. The difficult task of judging the English language poems was done by poets Frances Kakugawa, Anthony Quagliano, and Joseph Stanton. For the Japanese language poems, the haiku were judged by Uson Kanda of the Muteki Haiku

Club, Kiyoko Kanzaki of the Azami Haiku Club, Kozan Nishimura of the Shou-Kai Haiku Club, and Mitsuharu Shoji, editor of the *Hawaii Hochi* newspaper; while Kinue Freitas of the Odamaki Tanka Club, Tatsuo Teraoka of the Choon-shisha Tanka Club, and Jiro Nakano of the Ginu-shisha Tanka Club judged the tanka. With the judging completed, a final touch of grace and beauty was given by our two calligraphers, the Reverend Shoyei Hatta of Aiea Hongwanji Mission, Honolulu, who painted the characters on the cover, and Kazuaki Tanahashi, a well-known artist from San Francisco, who painted the characters that separate the book's sections.

Organizing the contest and judging the entries represented a considerable amount of work. However, we soon learned translation and production posed an even greater challenge. At this point, Dr. Nakano moved from being an invaluable adviser and enthusiastic supporter of our project to its main dynamo. He took in hand the enormous and arduous task of translating the Japanese poems into English. Joseph Stanton collaborated in the rendering of the poems in English. We at the Institute helped as much as we could, but the greater part of the burden fell directly upon Dr. Nakano's shoulders, who has done everything except turn the crank on the printing press. For all his work and dedication, we cannot thank him enough. Tatsuo Teraoka undertook the task of translating the English poems into Japanese, which Jiro Nakano, assuming yet a new role, reviewed. And, finally, John Haig of the University of Hawai'i's Japanese Department provided invaluable assistance with the bilingual word-processing programs.

In sum, as a result of the generosity and dedication of all those involved in the project, the Spark M. Matsunaga Institute for Peace is now able to present to the reader a thoughtful and provocative anthology of peace poetry, a collection that reflects the spirit of Senator Matsunaga's life and work as only poetry can.

Honolulu, 1995   Brien Hallett

平和詩歌集序言

　　　　この平和短歌俳句詩集は、機会に相応して必然的に成果されたものである。1986年（昭和61年）に創設されてから、松永平和研究所は、ハワイの生んだ米国合衆国上院議員、故スパーク松永氏の貢献に栄誉を与えようと努力してきた。1941年（昭和16年）、戦雲が暗く垂れこめてきたとき、ハワイ大学の一学生であった松永上院議員は、平和への知識と関心を刺激する為に米国国立平和学院大学を創立することを夢みていたと言われる。1981年（昭和56年）、彼の献身的な努力により、かって彼の見た夢が実現してきた。松永上院議員の提出した法案が両議院を通過し、米国政府の助成金によりハワイ大学平和研究所が創立された。松永上院議員の死後間もない1991年（平成3年）、ハワイ大学はハワイ大学平和研究所を松永平和研究所と改名した。この研究所を理想と情念に捧げて、我々の尊敬と敬意を表現したが、研究所に関係する人々の間に、何かもっと鮮明な実在的なものが必要であると感じられていた。

　　　　その機会がやってきた。1992年（平成4年）3月、私は、素晴らしい英訳歌集「Poets Behind Barbed Wire 鉄柵歌人」を買って読み、平和研究所の出版委員会（メンバー：ジャーナリズム学部教授トム・ブリスリン、大学図書館員ジョン・ハーク、ハワイ実業教育開発.旅行業学部教授リチャード・ジョウン、伝記研究センター教授ジョージ・シムソン、哲学部教授メリー・タイルズ、英文学部教授ブライアン・ハレット）に提出して皆にもそれを読んでもらった。その英訳歌集は、単にその中の短歌のすべてが優れているのみならず、歌われた環境がそれ以上に格別な意義があったのである。歌集の題名が、歌の鋭く迫力ある特性を表すのみか、戦時中、歌人達が監禁されていた収容所の廻りを取り囲む事実の鉄柵を顕示している。タール紙を貼ったバラックに住んでいた、これらの日系米国人の歌人等は彼等の監禁生活の酷悪な奇運を、詩歌のみ表現が可能である痛痕で直裁的な方法で書きあげたのである。

　　　　この「Poets Behind Barbed Wire」を読んだ後、研究所の出版委員会の他の委員達は皆、平和に関するバイリングアル（日本語.英語）詩歌集を出版し、それを故松永上院議員に捧げることが最も適切で明白なへの賛辞であると言う私の提言に賛成してくれた。

　　　　また、委員会の全ては、芸術一般、特に詩による表現が、いかに強烈に、肯定的に平和を促進することが出

来るかを信じていたから、この事業を異常な熱狂的同意を
もって支援した。いろいろな文化的背景の詩人達が詩歌コ
ンテストに応募したことは、この混乱する世界に生きてい
る我々の平和と理解を相互に深求することに貢献し、また
促進するものであると思う。その上、我々の全ては、詩と
平和の組み合わせが、どんなによく故松永上院議員の生涯
の貢献を要約するであろうかと確信した。なぜなら、松永
氏は、平和のためにたゆみなく働く人であったと同時に、
この書の序に記載された彼の詩に見られるように、氏は、
生前、窮地に追われた人間の神秘性を熟考しつつ、しばし
ば詩を書いて自らの深い心情を表現した。

　この詩歌集出版事業を発足するために、私は、最
初のインスピレーションを与えてくれた人．医師中野次郎
氏に連絡した。彼は、歌集「Poets Behind Barbed Wire」
を編集、英訳した人である。ヒロ在住の医師.歌人の中野
先生は、親切にも、ホノルルに飛来し、出版委員会の委員
達と合うことを同意して下さった。中野氏は、ながらく英
語の短詩（俳句）を書いているホノルルの教育者且つ詩人
であるフランシス・カクガワ氏とダロルド．ブライダ氏に
来てもらい、彼等の詩作の知識と経験からこの事業に関与
する意見を求めることを強く勧められた。直ちに、二人の
詩人に電話で連絡すると、快く会合に出席することを受諾
して下さった。私達は、平和研究所の会議室で初めて会っ
たとき、バイリングアルな詩歌集出版が、松永上院議員に
栄誉を与えるに最もふさわしい事業であると同意した。更
に、平和研究所が平和を主題とした詩歌のコンテストとし
て、俳句と短歌を日本語で募集することに同意し、平和研
究所編集員スタンレー．シャップ氏は、一九九二年、直ち
にコンテストを編成する計画をたてることにした。

　この詩歌コンテストに応募した日本、ハワイ、合
衆国本土、カナダ、ブラジル、英国等、一七七人の詩人の
約八〇〇の俳句、短歌が寄稿され、その中から、平和研究
所出版委員会の指名した選者により最後の入選詩歌が決定
された。英語俳句を審査する困難な仕事は、詩人フランシ
ス・．カクガワ、詩人.文学批評家アントニー・カグリア
ノ教授、並びにハワイ大学芸術人文学センター部長.ジョ
セフ・スタントン教授に指名された。日本語俳句の選者は、
霧笛俳句会の神田烏村、あざみ俳句会の神崎清子、蕉雨会
の西村虹山、ハワイ報知編集長庄司光伯がなり、短歌の選
者には、おだまき短歌会のフレイタス絹恵、潮音詩社の寺

岡達夫と銀雨詩社の中野次郎がなった。入選俳句並びに短
歌が決定した後、アイエア本願寺の住職で書道家八田昭永
師が表題を書き、サンフランシスコの有名な棚橋一昭が各
俳句、短歌を日本語で最後の優実. 優雅な筆で書き終えた。
　　　詩歌の募集. コンテスト並びに応募された作品の
審査には並々ならぬ労力であった。しかし、それ以上、入
選句、入選歌の翻訳と編集には、非常に困難な挑戦が待ち
受けていた。この大きな難業を完遂する為に、中野先生は、
評価出来ないほど良きアドバイザーとして、また情熱的な
実行者としてダイナモのように働いてくださった。彼は、
入選した日本語の俳句、短歌のすべてを英訳し、又英語の
俳句を日本語訳するなど非常に骨の折れる仕事をしてくだ
さり、すぐ出版出来るようなワープロ・ソフトディスクの
コピーまでも製作して下さった。ジョセフ・スタントン教
授並びに平和研究所の我々は、中野先生の英訳俳句、短歌
をさらに検詩編集し、歌集の最後のフォームを完成した。
しかし、最大の重責は、何と言っても中野先生の両肩に直
接かかり、印刷機を動かす以外のすべてが彼によりなされ
たと言えよう。我々は、彼のたゆまざる大業に深く感謝し、
言葉では十分述べ切れない思いである。一方、寺岡達夫氏
は、英語の短詩を日本語に訳すことに心労を尽くし、中野
次郎氏は、更にこれらの訳された詩の再吟味する新役を遂
行された。そして、最後に、ハワイ大学日本語学部のジョ
ン・ヘイグ氏がバイリンガルのワープロ・プログラムを駆
使して、この詩歌集のプリントを完成する貴重な援助をし
てくださった。
　　　終りに、この事業は多くの人々が専心的な援助と
尽力をしてくださった賜であることに感謝したい。平和研
究所は、故松永上院議員のライフ・ワークの精神を反映す
べき、平和を主題した深慮的且つ挑発的な詩歌集を出版し、
ここに読者に贈るものである。

ハワイ・ホノルルにて

　　　松永平和研究所長ハワイ大学英文学部教授
ブライアン・ハレット

Peace Tanka in Japanese

平和短歌

山々は
遥か霞みて
藤棚の
花見る人等
皆優しかり

Mountains are misty
in the distance;
all viewers
of wisteria blossoms
are gentle and graceful.

yamayama wa
haruka kasumite
fujidana no
hanamiru hitora
mina yasashikari

原野とみえ
ホノルル

Tomie Harano
Honolulu, Hawai'i

3

空港の
車椅子なる
松永氏
温和な笑顔
見おさめとなり

The airport
was the last place
we saw the gently smiling face
of Senator Matsunaga
in a wheelchair.

kuko no
kurumaisu naru
matsunaga-shi
onwana egao
miosame to nari

東清子
ホノルル

Kiyoko Higashi
Honolulu, Hawai'i

4

群あそぶ
小鳩の姿
平和なり
あまねく光
わが庭に満つ

How peaceful
the little doves playing
in a group—
my garden everywhere
suffused with sunlight!

mure asobu
kobato no sugata
heiwa nari
amaneku hikari
waga niwa ni mitsu

平林三八子
ホノルル

Miyako Hirabayashi
Honolulu, Hawai'i

5

管制が
取れて明るき
街の中
顔も輝く
終戦の夜

The blackout is over!
On the brightened street
every face is
illuminated—
the night of the end of the war.

kansei ga
torete akaruki
machi no naka
kao mo kagayaku
shusen no yoru

黄雪英
ラプエンテ

Sei Eng Huang
La Puente, California

戦いの
悲惨は子等に
教うべし
世人は希う
尊き平和

We shall teach
the children
of war's miseries
because humanity must hope
for the priceless peace.

tatakai no
hisan wa kora ni
oshiu beshi
sejin wa negau
totoki heiwa

亀田佳子
パール・シティ

Yoshiko Kameda
Pearl City, Hawai'i

7

戦争を
知らぬ世代に
原爆の
惨を語らむ
生あるかぎり

To the end of our lives,
we shall tell of the horrors
of the atomic bombing
to the generations
that were not there.

senso wo
shiranu sedai ni
genbaku no
san wo kataran
sei aru kagiri

加藤紀子
ホノルル

Michiko Kato
Honolulu, Hawai'i

原始林
開きし斧音
はるかにて
今平穏の
ボール打つ音

The sounds of the axes
that opened the virgin forests
have faded away.
Now one hears the hitting
of baseball bats.

genshirin
hirakishi fuon
haruka nite
ima heion no
boru utsu oto

加藤喜代子
ロンドリナ、ブラジル

Kiyoko Kato
Londrina, Brazil

9

戦いて
帰らぬ人の
忠魂碑
苔むすままに
草に埋もれり

For the soldiers
who went to war
and never returned,
a moss-laden monument
is buried in the grass.

tatakaite
kaeranu hito no
chukonhi
kokemusu mamani
kusa ni umoreri

桐沢茂
新潟

Shigeru Kirisawa
Niigata, Japan

10

数知れぬ
異人種移りて
ブラジルに
一つの平和に
手をつなぎたり

A farrago
of races
migrated to Brazil,
holding hands
in a singular peace.

kazu shirenu
ijinshu utsurite
burajiru ni
hitotsu no heiwa ni
te wo tsunagi tari

岡本喜代子
サンパオロ、ブラジル

Kiyoko Okamoto
Sao Paulo, Brazil

11

夫婦して
狭き畑に
背を丸め
種を蒔く手に
土やわらかし

A farmer couple bending
their backs to sow the seeds
in a narrow patch;
the hands are soft
to the touch.

fufu shite
semaki hatake ni
se wo marume
tane wo maku te ni
tsuchi yawarakashi

小泉一美
バークレー

Kazumi Koizumi
Berkeley, California

人は逝き
世は移れども
悠久の
陽は今日も出で
われらを照らす

The man has passed away
and the era changes,
but an eternal sun
appears again today,
shining.

hito wa yuki
yo wa utsure domo
yukyu no
hi wa kyo mo ide
warera wo terasu

小西文子
ホノルル

Fumiko Konishi
Honolulu, Hawai'i

争ひも
不足も知らぬ
水鳥の
番いを見つつ
岸辺に憩う

Resting on the shore,
I am watching
paired ducks glide,
unaware of struggle
and discontent.

arasoi mo
fusoku mo shiranu
mizudori no
tsugai wo mitsutsu
kishibe ni ikou

徐奇壁
ハシエンダ・ハイト

In Pi Lai
Hacienda Heights, California

土に生き
土に還らん
農夫われ
耕す土に
平和育てん

I, a farmer,
living on earth,
to return to earth,
shall nurture peace
by tilling the soil.

tsuchi ni iki
tsuchi ni kaeran
nofu ware
tagayasu tsuchini
heiwa sodaten

箕輪新七
ロンドリナ、ブラジル

Shinshiti Minowa
Londrina, Brazil

15

ソマリヤの
子等の目は皆
悲しくて
訴え続く
テレビに今日も

The pitiful eyes
of the children
in Somalia
continue their appeal
on TV again today.

somariya no
kora no me wa mina
kanashikute
uttae tsuzuku
terebi ni kyo

三浦とし枝
ワヒアワ

Toshie Miura
Wahiawa, Hawai'i

老いの身の
只出来る事と
祈るなり
世界の平和を
夜明けと共に

I am old.
All I can do
is pray for peace
for the world
at this sunrise.

oi no mi no
tada dekiru koto to
inoru nari
sekai no heiwa wo
yoake to tomo ni

森田不二子
ホノルル

Fujiko Morita
Honolulu, Hawai'i

17

太平洋
平和の風に
波静か
茜の色に
今日も暮れゆく

The Pacific Ocean
has its breeze of peace
and tranquil waves,
but, staining the sky madder red,
today comes to an end.

taiheiyo
heiwa no kaze ni
nami shizuka
akane no iro ni
kyo mo kureyuku

村田ヘンリー
サクラメント

Henry Murata
Sacramento, California

反戦歌
いづこの国より
鳴り響く
空に向って
我も口ずさむ

This antiwar song,
from which country
does it come?
I am also humming
toward the sky.

hansenka
izuko no kuni yori
nari hibiku
sora ni mukatte
ware mo kuchizusamu

中原トシミ
リバーリッジ

Toshimi Nakahara
River Edge, New Jersey

ものみなの
生命しと
知る時に
小さき虫さえ
愛しかりける

Perceiving
every creature has a life,
we see even
the tiniest insect
is lovable.

mono mina no
inochi shito
shiru toki ni
chiisaki mushi sae
kanashi karikeru

中西美沙
ホノルル

Misa Nakanishi
Honolulu, Hawai'i

20

落日の
浜辺に立てば
聞こえくる
平和を希う
わだつみの声

As I stand
on the beach at sunset,
I can hear
the voices of the ocean
crying for peace.

rakujitsu no
hamabe ni tateba
kikoe kuru
heiwa wo negau
wadatsumi no koe

中西美沙
ホノルル

Misa Nakanishi
Honolulu, Hawai'i

反核の
デモに列なる
主婦の背に
こんこんと眠る
みどり児の顔

How innocent a face!
The baby sleeping soundly
on the back of the mother
marching with
the antinuke demonstration.

hankaku no
demo ni tsuranaru
shufu no se ni
konkon to nemuru
midorigo no kao

中野次郎
ヒロ

Jiro Nakano
Hilo, Hawai'i

地球人
みな同胞と
相おもい
相いつくしむ
世界創造らな

All earthlings
are created
to consider how all
are compatriots of love
and helping.

chikyujin
mina harakara to
ai omoi
ai itsukushimu
sekai tsukurana

野島泰子
東京

Hiroko Nojima
Tokyo, Japan

23

白・黒・黄
皮膚の違ひを
真底に
君は納得
せむやせざるや

Do you consent—
all peoples white, black, and yellow—
to your differences
of surface
to the bottoms of your hearts?

shiro kuro ki
hifu no chigai wo
shinzoko ni
kimi wa nattoku
senya sezaruya

大西秋佳
川西市

Shuka Onishi
Kawanishi, Japan

24

アメリカに
生れし吾子ゆえ
日米の
かけ橋となれ
次世紀の世に

My child,
born in America,
you shall be a bridge
between Japan and the U.S.A.
for the next century.

amerika ni
areshi ako yue
nichibei no
kakehashi to nare
jiseiki no yo ni

岡田明子
アナハイム

Akiko Okada
Anaheim, California

25

それぞれに
国と民族
違えども
平和のシンボル
白鳩は飛ぶ

Despite differences
between
countries and races,
white birds fly
as symbols of peace.

sorezore ni
kuni to minzoku
chigae domo
heiwa no shinboru
shirahato wa to

岡崎猪三喜
サウス・ゲイト

Isaki Okazaki
South Gate, California

26

次の代を
担う若人
手をとりて
鳴らせよ地球の
平和の鐘を

Young men,
carrying the next century,
walk hand in hand,
clanging the bell of peace
all over the earth.

tsugi no yo wo
ninau wakodo
te wo torite
narase yo chikyu no
heiwa no kane wo

セイブル圭子
タコマ

Kayko S. Seible
Tacoma, Washington

平和なぞ
叫びつ裏で
人殺す
武器を作りて
富む国のあり

You cry out
loudly for peace
but earn a fortune
selling arms
that kill.

Heiwa nazo
sakebitsu ura de
hito korosu
buki wo tsukurite
tomu kuni no ari

瀬古義信
ロンドリナ

Yoshinobu Seko
Londrina, Brazil

28

戦争の
孤児の名背負ひ
さまよいし
悲しみ今も
老いのこの身に

I have roamed the streets
carrying the name
"war orphan";
even now sorrows
reside in my old body.

senso no
koji no na seoi
samayoishi
kanashimi imamo
oi no kono mi ni

ストリッチ前田テイコ
キシミー

Teiko Maeda Stritch
Kissimmee, Florida

いくさ無き
平和を希う
松永の
遺訓を称う
除隊兵われは

We veterans
laud the legacy
left by Senator Matsunaga:
an earnest desire
for no more war.

ikusa naki
heiwa wo negau
matsunaga no
ikun wo tatau
jotaihei ware wa

寺岡達夫
パール・シティ

Tatsuo Teraoka
Pearl City, Hawai'i

長き病い
癒えて弾める
出勤路
虹輝ける
下くぐりゆく

Recovered
from a long illness
excitedly I go to work
under the brilliant rainbow
arched above the commuting road.

nagaki yamai
iete hazumeru
shukkinji
niji kagayakeru
shita kuguri yuku

時任愛子
ホノルル

Aiko Tokito
Honolulu, Hawai'i

31

共生の
青き地球を
慈しみ
人類の歴史よ
平和であれと

Loving the blue earth
we live together
hoping the history
of humankind
will be peaceful forever.

kyosei no
aoki chikyu wo
itsukushimi
jinrui no rekishi yo
heiwa de are to

上原あつ子
ホノルル

Atsuko Uyehara
Honolulu, Hawai'i

炎天の
平和の鳩を
追ひながら
幼児鳩の
言葉をつかふ

Inadvertently,
my baby uses the words
of the peaceful pigeons,
while chasing them
under a blazing sun.

enten no
heiwa no hato wo
oi nagara
osanago hato no
kotoba wo tsukau

前川博
千葉

Hiroshi Maekawa
Chiba, Japan

33

太平洋に
向きて咲きいる
浜なすの
実は白々と
潮騒をきく

They bloom near
all Pacific shores—
oh, sweet briars
of the pale fruits—
as we hear the sound of the waves.

taiheiyo ni
mukite sakiiru
hamanasu no
mi wa shirajira to
shiosai wo kiku

東郷しずえ
東京

Shizue Togo
Tokyo, Japan

恵まるる
日々の平和の
有難さ
揺るがぬ国に
住めば安けし

Blessed be peace
from day to day,
I am grateful
to be living content
in a stable country.

megumaruru
hibi no heiwa no
arigata sa
yuruganu kuni ni
sumeba yasukeshi

松田淑子
ホノルル

Yoshiko Matsuda
Honolulu, Hawai'i

35

春雨は
木の芽を濡らし
石を濡らし
人の心に
平和もたらす

Spring rain gently
soaks tree buds
and stones
bringing
peace to the heart.

harusame wa
ki no me wo nurashi
ishi wo nurashi
hito no kokoro ni
heiwa motarasu

松田淑子
ホノルル

Yohiko Matsuda
Honolulu, Hawai'i

国々の
言葉も衣服も
異なれど
平和を希ふ
心はひとつ

Though each nation
differs in language
and dress,
all desire
the same peace on earth.

kuniguni no
kotoba mo ifuku mo
kotonaredo
heiwa wo negau
kokoro wa hitotsu

フレイタス絹恵
ホノルル

Kinue Freitas
Honolulu, Hawai'i

東西の
雪の溶けしに
経済の
摩擦は平和を
うすくそぎゆく

East and West
the snow has melted away,
but money matters
diminish
world peace.

tozai no
yuki wa tokete mo
keizai no
masatsu wa heiwa wo
usuku sogiyuku

田中重代
ホノルル

Shigeyo Tanaka
Honolulu, Hawai'i

孫達へ
二十一世紀を
贈りたし
平和を祈る
リボン結びて

To my grandchildren,
I wish to present
the twenty-first century
tied with a ribbon—
a prayer for peace.

magotachi e
nijuisseiki wo
okuritashi
heiwa wo inoru
ribon musubite

マスグローブ羊子
ホノルル

Yoko Musglove
Honolulu, Hawai'i

書き初めに
「平和な国」と
書く子等の
無心いとしむ
元旦の朝

New Year's morning;
children innocently write
peaceful nation
as the first calligraphy
of the year.

kakizome ni
heiwa no kuni to
kaku kora no
mushin itoshimu
gantan no asa

中川雅子
ワヒアワ

Masako Nakagawa
Wahiawa, Hawai'i

40

文明の
進化に較べ
人類の
真の平和は
いずこに行きし

World civilization
may be progressing,
but where in the world
has true peace
gone?

bunmei no
shinka ni kurabe
jinrui no
shin no heiwa wa
izuko ni yukishi

池村早苗
ホノルル

Sanae Ikemura
Honolulu, Hawai'i

41

平和とふ
言葉うつろな
響きあり
今日も弾丸とぶ
サラエボの空

The word *peace*:
how hollow and empty
it rings by itself!
Today shells are still flying
in the sky of Sarajevo.

heiwa chou
kotoba utsuro na
hibiki ari
kyo mo tama tobu
saraebo no sora

太田孝子
ホノルル

Takako Ota
Honolulu, Hawai'i

地球儀を
まはせば飢餓と
戦争の
繰り返し見ゆ
愛する地球に

Turning a globe,
I wonder why
our beloved earth
continues to repeat
only starvation and war.

chikyugi wo
mawaseba kiga to
senso no
kurikaeshi miyu
aisuru chikyu ni

太田孝子
ホノルル

Takako Ota
Honolulu, Hawai'i

43

ひたぶるに
声なき児等の
祈りとふ
黄色きリボン
校舎彩る

The school buildings
are colored with
yellow ribbons—
the earnest prayers
of voiceless children.

hitaburu ni
koe naki kora no
inori chou
kiiroki ribon
kosha irodoru

清水聖子
ホノルル

Seiko Shimizu
Honolulu, Hawai'i

降りそそぐ
光の粒を
浴びながら
群れ踊る児らは
平和の使者か

As they bathe,
the falling drops
glistening in the sun—
the dancing children are
messengers of peace.

furisosogu
hikari no tsubu wo
abinagara
mure odoru kora wa
heiwa no shisha ka

山本良子
ホノルル

Yoshiko Yamamoto
Honolulu, Hawai'i

一人が
心の平静
保つとき
そこに生まるる
宇宙の平和

When every person
keeps his peace
of mind,
universal peace
will be born.

ichinin ga
kokoro no heisei
tamotsu toki
soko ni umaruru
uchu no heiwa

山本良子
ホノルル

Yoshiko Yamamoto
Honolulu, Hawai'i

46

平等に
コスモポリタン
歩みいる
ハワイ州こそ
平和の島ぞ

Cosmopolitans
walk hand in hand
as equals:
truly our state of Hawai'i
is the island of peace.

byodo ni
kosumoporitan
ayumi iru
hawaishu koso
heiwa no shima zo

新里縫子
パール・シティ

Nuiko Shinsato
Pearl City, Hawai'i

47

ハワイにて
二十年平和に
過したり
人の情を
あまた受けつつ

For twenty years
peacefully I have lived
my life in Hawai'i,
receiving abundantly
the love of others.

hawai nite
nijunen heiwa ni
sugoshitari
hito no nasake wo
amata uketsutsu

鈴木志津子
ホノルル

Shizuko Suzuki
Honolulu, Hawai'i

48

幼な児の
母に抱かれ
眠りいる
世にも平和な
姿に見あかず

A tiny baby
is in its mother's arms—
a peaceful scene
I could watch
forever.

osanago no
haha ni idakare
nemuri iru
yo nimo heiwa na
shi ni miakazu

高原政子
ワヒアワ

Masako Takahara
Wahiawa, Hawai'i

49

月までも
旅する人の
ある世にて
尚も遠きか
世界平和は

Though we have
travelled to the moon,
world peace
is still too far away
to reach.

tsuki made mo
tabisuru hito no
aru yo nite
naomo toki ka
sekai heiwa wa

森川静江
ホノルル

Shizue Morikawa
Honolulu, Hawai'i

50

頭を垂れて
ひたすら何にか
熱中の
吾児のうなじに
春の陽やさし

Bending his head,
my child is engrossed
in something;
his nape gleams
in the gentle spring sun.

zu wo tarete
hitasura nani ka
necchu no
ako no unaji ni
haru no hi yasashi

桝谷佳織
ホノルル

Kaori Masutani
Honolulu, Hawai'i

平和なる
朝の出勤
信号待ち
見上ぐる空に
残月淡し

Peaceful morning,
on the way to work,
I await the green light—
the pale moon floats
in the sky.

heiwa naru
asa no shukkin
shingo machi
miaguru sora ni
zangetsu awashi

滝田裕子
ホノルル

Yuko Takita
Honolulu, Hawai'i

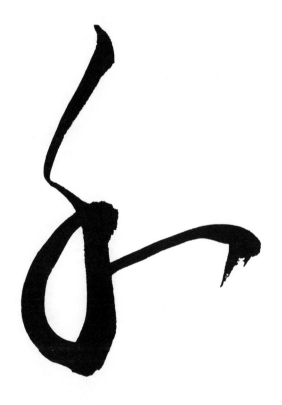

Peace Poetry in English

平和英語詩歌集

false teeth
frozen in the glass
the cold

グラス中
入歯も凍る
寒さかな

Winona Baker
Nanaimo, British Columbia

two separate forms
rigid in the double bed
a quarrel between

ダブルベッド
いさかいかたくな
影二つ

Winona Baker
Nanaimo, British Columbia

broken cup
still holds much water
for sparrows

毀れても
コップに残る
鳥の水

Jim Bernath
Littleton, Colorado

the soldiers hide
their poems
what are they really
afraid of?

軍人の
怖れは何ぞ
詩を胸に

Jim Bernath
Littleton, Colorado

58

foot disturbs the moon pool
playful   beyond
  this ocean   war

水遊び
プールの満月
毀わされる

Jim Bernath
Littleton, Colorado

high mountain valley
made of white light
the trees try to approach

山深く
木々とも包む
白光の朝

Nik Bernath
Littleton, Colorado

morning fog:
feeling the mountains
without seeing

霧の朝
山は触れ合う
見えずとも

Nik Bernath
Littleton, Colorado

dead of winter
cemetery in the dark
wild geese sleeping there

冬探し
暗き墓場に
鴨の宿

Nik Bernath
Littleton, Colorado

Hiroshima heat—
mother and daughter
fold a thousand cranes

千羽鶴
母と娘が折る
広島の夏

Margaret Chula
Portland, Oregon

where does
the waterfall begin
and where does it end
the koi
swim in a circle

瀧壺に
鯉はぐるぐる
めぐりおり

Margaret Chula
Portland, Oregon

as the sun rises
a dove flies across the sea
with dew on her wings
from newly opened blossoms
the drip-dripping of spring rain

鳩一羽
朝日にはばたき
春雨に花散る如く
海原をゆく

Margaret Chula
Portland, Oregon

solitary crane
embroidered on my pillow
brings dreams of Japan
the winter cranes of Kyushu
and origami peace chains

刺繍せし
鶴の枕に休らえば
平和を祈りつ
九州の顕つ

Margaret Chula
Portland, Oregon

shoulder to shoulder
a pair of cooing doves leaves
no room for quarrels

番い鳩
いさかいもなし
肩と肩

Lyllian Cole
Victoria, British Columbia

August sunshine
all the children drop their guns
for lemonade

炎天下
玩具の銃より
レモネード

Carol Dagenhardt
Abingdon, Maryland

how slowly
the heron's wings rise and fall
stroking the air

鷺の羽
ゆるり上下の
空に絵を

David Elliott
Factoryville, Pennsylvania

not expecting
such a moon
over my crabby neighbor's roof

名月や
うるさき隣家の
屋根の上

David Elliott
Factoryville, Pennsylvania

peace talk
under the table
socks that don't match

靴下の
色まちまち
平和会議

LeRoy Gorman
Napanee, Ontario

Cold War over
the poet and his translator
cross over to yell at each other

冷戦逝き
詩人と訳者は
いがみ合い

LeRoy Gorman
Napanee, Ontario

the peacetime airshow
birds whitewash
the bombers

平和時エア・ショウ
鳥等は爆撃機を
白く塗り

LeRoy Gorman
Napanee, Ontario

opaque water
catalpa leaf drifting by
folded on itself

濁水に
カタルパの美れい
流さるる

Yvonne Hardenbrook
Murrysville, Pennsylvania

mountain meadow
a tranquil stream mending
the jagged halves

野雲雀は
せせらぐ河に
癒される

Yvonne Hardenbrook
Murrysville, Pennsylvania

the very same sleeves
that once caught bitter tears
folded now for tea

茶の席に
涙しごきし
同じ袖

Yvonne Hardenbrook
Murrysville, Pennsylvania

sunset streaks the sky—
a late hawk hurries nestward
toward a peaceful night;

along the edge of the waves
a single sandpiper plays

夕暮れに
平和の巣へと
急ぐ鷹

波ぎわに
一羽の鴫は
遊ぶなり

Lorraine Harr
Portland, Oregon

Kid says, "No way!" Mom
says, "Just do it!" And Grandma
says, "Negotiate."

子は否と
母実行
祖母協調

Ryan Hirasuna
Honolulu, Hawai'i

Good Friday
all day snow brings memories
of last Christmas Eve

受苦日の
降雪に憶えり
クリスマス・イブ

Jean Jorgensen
Edmonton, Alberta

utter calm
of the old country cemetery
from where I stand
honeybees fly in and out
of the broken church window

故里の静まる墓地に
佇めば
蜜蜂飛び交う
教会の窓

Jean Jorgensen
Edmonton, Alberta

afternoon visit
to the Japanese Gardens
this morning's quarrel
forgotten now as we stand
hand in hand before Buddha

昼下がり
日本庭園訪ね来て
いさかい消ゆる
佛像の前

Jean Jorgensen
Edmonton, Alberta

Red Cross Nurse
uses the surrender flag
as a tourniquet

赤十字婦
止血に白旗を
使いたり

Jim Kacian
Berryville, Virginia

empty temple—
the plain-dressed monk bows
to the silence

空き寺に
黙礼捧げん
通り僧

Jim Kacian
Berryville, Virginia

Hand in hand they stand
In silence; a smile, a nod.
Peace has no language.

握手しつ
沈黙、微笑、会釈、
平和に言語なし

Frances Kakugawa
Honolulu, Hawai'i

remaining snow . . .
half the birds flying
half nesting

残雪や
飛ぶ鳥もあり
巣篭るもあり

Donald Kelly
Evergreen Park, Illinois

after the shelling
a priest glues the dove of peace
back together

傷つきし
平和の鳩に
牧師の看護

Elizabeth Searle Lamb
Sante Fe, New Mexico

the hot air balloon
shaped like a dove rises—
the cloudless sky

晴天に
鳩のごと昇る
熱気球

Elizabeth Searle Lamb
Sante Fe, New Mexico

starving child—
what do flies find to eat
on her eyelids . . .

飢餓の児の
まぶたに蠅は
食探す

Leatrice Lifshitz
Pomona, New York

88

several wars later
the black cannon pointing
at pink dogwood

幾戦後
みずきに向かう
大砲黒し

Leatrice Lifshitz
Pomona, New York

at the inn
Christmas lights strung between
cannon

大砲を
飾れる宿に
クリスマスの灯

Leatrice Lifshitz
Pomona, New York

the old warrior
by his fallen soldier son
broke his ancient sword

老武将
吾子の戦死に
古刀割る

Jerry Lightfoot
Garland, Texas

green/brass shell casing
in the new jungle—now home
to a hermit crab

弾殻は
新たにかわる
やどかりの宿

Jerry Lightfoot
Garland, Texas

reading poetry
in the light of the shellburst
that took his young life

弾光に
詩を読み逝きし
若き武士

Jerry Lightfoot
Garland, Texas

in his pocket
the camera without lens
chaplain in the rain

レンズ無き
カメラ手に軍僧
雨の中

Lenard D. Moore
Raleigh, North Carolina

deepening winter—
the sound
of UN trucks

国連の
ドラック響く
冬真中

Lenard D. Moore
Raleigh, North Carolina

peacekeeping—
mail call in Somalia
divorce papers

ソマリヤの
治安励む兵に
離婚届け

Nika
Calgary , Alberta

Vietnam vet
seeking a lasting peace
suicide note

ベトナム除隊兵
永遠の平和に
遺書残す

Nika
Calgary , Alberta

sand castles
becoming
sand

砂の城
やがては帰る
元の砂

Nika
Calgary, Alberta

thunder rolls across
the wooded hills; in sunlight
a hidden wren calls

雷去りて
静まる樹間に
鷦鷯鳴く

Dylan Pugh
Leicestershire, England

in Gauguin's hut
his last picture
Breton snow

ゴーガンの
部屋に残せし絵
ブレトンの雪

Anthony Quagliano
Honolulu, Hawai'i

the baby reaching
for the snowflakes falling from
the bomberless sky

空爆なき日
落つ雪片掴む
幼児の手

Kohin Sakamoto
Kyoto, Japan

peace conference . . .
floating to the windowsill
the white feather

平和会議
白き羽毛浮かぶ
窓の辺に

Elizabeth St Jacques
Sault Ste. Marie, Ontario

together
in the sun
potted roses and bonsai

柔ら陽に
盆栽と薔薇
融和して

Elizabeth St Jacques
Sault Ste. Marie, Ontario

out the back window
the thrush sang greenery light
and blue-note shadow—
as if the burning cities
were only evening news teams

夕闇に鶫の
歌の窓越しに
青と緑の冴ゆる調よ

Joseph Stanton
Honolulu, Hawai'i

my letters
to a Croatian friend
lost in a battlefield

文届かず
クロアチアの友は
戦場下

Kenneth Tanemura
Redwood City, California

sunshine on the flag
hand on the Bible
the president promises

星條旗
大統領誓う
聖書手に

Nina A. Wicker
Sanford, North Carolina

New Year's Day
ant and yellowjacket sip
the same bread crumb

元旦や
パン屑を咬む
蜂と蟻

Nina A. Wicker
Sanford, North Carolina

Peace Haiku in Japanese

平和俳句

留学生と
片言づつの
良夜かな

A foreign student
Speaking faltering sentences . . .
A moonlit night!

ryugakusei to
katagoto zutsu no
ryoya kana

荒谷きく
北海道

Kiku Araya
Mashikecho, Hokkaido

111

ホームステイ
終えて涙の
涼しさよ

The last day
of the homestay . . .
refreshing tears!

homustei
oete namida no
suzushisa yo

荒谷きく
北海道

Kiku Araya
Mashikecho, Hokkaido

憂いなく
生くる平和や
春麗

Without worry,
living in peace . . .
beautiful spring!

urei naku
ikuru heiwa ya
haru urara

越後谷義一
北海道

Giichi Echigoya
Eijumashike, Hokkaido

生くるもの
命尊し
母子草

For all that lives
life is precious—
mother-child grass*!

ikuru mono
inochi totoshi
hahakogusa

(*cottonweed)

越後谷義一
北海道

Giichi Echigoya
Eijumashike, Hokkaido

日系も
明るく育ち
桃の花

Japanese-Americans
also growing happily;
plums blossom.

nikkei mo
akaruku sodachi
momo no hana

藤広松於
カルバー・シティ

Matsuo Fujihiro
Culver City, California

115

原爆の
悪夢も覚めて
若菜摘む

Awakening from a bad dream
of the atomic bomb,
I gather young herbs.

genbaku no
akumu mo samete
wakana tsumu

黄雪英
ラプエンテ

Sei Eng Huang
La Puente, California

師の墓に
サンキュウ言えば
河鹿鳴く

As I say "Thank you"
at my teacher's tomb,
a frog starts croaking.

shi no haka ni
sankyu ieba
kajika naku

伊牟田忠敏
ロング・ビーチ

Tadatoshi Imuta
Long Beach, California

春の空
元気にパレード
４４２

Spring sky . . .
parading in high spirits,
the 442nd Regiment.

haru no sora
genki ni paredo
fo-fo-tsu

井上和子
ホノルル

Kazuko Inoue
Honolulu, Hawai'i

国連旗
はためき和み
風薫る

The UN flag
fluttering calmly
in the fragrant breeze.

kokurenki
hatameki nagomi
kaze kaoru

神田烏村
ホノルル

Uson Kanda
Honolulu, Hawai'i

踊る輪に
観る輪に異人
島の盆

A ring of dancers:
a ring of *ijin** watchers—
Bon Festival in the islands.

odoru wa ni
miru wa ni ijin
shima no bon

(*non-Japanese)

神崎清子
ホノルル

Kiyoko Kanzaki
Honolulu, Hawai'i

盆踊り
五世のかざす
もみじの手

Bon dance;
a *gosei** shading his eyes
with a tiny hand.

bon odori
gosei no kazasu
momiji no te

(* fifth Japanese generation)

川本雪恵
ホノルル

Yukie Kawamoto
Honolulu, Hawai'i

夏日燦
二世の武勲
永久に

Summer sun shining . . .
a nisei's war service
distinguished forever.

natsubi san
nisei no bukun
eikyu ni

川本雪恵
ホノルル

Yukie Kawamoto
Honolulu, Hawai'i

122

移民史に
秘めし平和や
風薫る

Hidden peace
in the immigrants' history . . .
fragrant breeze!

iminshi ni
himeshi heiwa ya
kaze kaoru

川野富美
ホノルル

Fumi Kawano
Honolulu, Hawai'i

123

移民塚に
眠る歴史や
風涼し

In immigrant's grave,
history sleeps . . .
a refreshing breeze rises.

iminzuka ni
nemuru rekishi ya
kaze suzushi

川野富美
ホノルル

Fumi Kawano
Honolulu, Hawai'i

124

平安の
一日なりけり
根深汁

How peaceful
this day is passing . . .
spring onion soup!

heian no
hitohi narikeri
nebuka-jiru

岸並信子
ホノルル

Nobuko Kishinam
Honolulu, Hawai'i

万緑や
お茶がとりもつ
日布の和

A myriad of green leaves!
Tea mediates a harmony
between Japan and Hawai'i

banryoku ya
ocha ga torimotsu
nippu no wa

北島光枝
ホノルル

Mitsue Kitajima
Honolulu, Hawai'i

手をつなぎ
和の輪を広げ
盆ダンス

Bon dance—
the ring of harmony widens
with hands joining each other.

te wo tsunagi
wa no wa wo hiroge
bon dansu

北島光枝
ホノルル

Mitsue Kitajima
Honolulu, Hawai'i

平和の鐘
ひびけ夏空の
果てまでも

Peace Bell—
ring it to the end
of the summer sky!

heiwa no kane
hibike natsuzora no
hate made mo

小谷凡味留
ヒロ

Bonmiru Kodani
Hilo, Hawai'i

ケアの嶺に
兆す平和の
初明り

Mauna Kea summit—
New Year sunrise shows
the sign of peace.

kea no ne ni
kizasu heiwa no
hatsu akari

小出月梢
ヒロ

Gessho Koide
Hilo, Hawai'i

山麓の
キャンプ静けし
初夏の朝

Early summer morning—
the camps are tranquil
at the mountain foothills.

sanroku no
kyanpu shizukeshi
shoka no asa

小出月梢
ヒロ

Gessho Koide
Hilo, Hawai'i

初夏の島
平和に明くる
老の幸

Early summer in the islands
day breaking peacefully—
the happiness of aging.

shoka no shima
heiwa ni akuru
oi no sachi

小出月梢
ヒロ

Gessho Koide
Hilo, Hawai'i

平和の鐘
鳴らし続けむ
秋の空

Autumn sky—
I shall keep ringing
the Peace Bell.

heiwa no kane
nashitsuzuken
aki no sora

桑田晃
京都

Hikaru Kuwada
Kyoto, Japan

春の雲
けなげに生きるも
平和なり

Spring cloud . . .
it is a peace
to live heroically.

haru no kumo
kenageni ikiru mo
heiwa nari

松谷夏
神奈川

Natsu Matsutani
Kanagawa, Japan

真珠湾に
平和の春の
波静か

Pearl Harbor—
the waves are calm
in peaceful spring

shinjuwan ni
heiwa no haru no
nami shizuka

箕輪新七
ロンドリナ、ブラジル

Shinshita Minowa
Londrina, Brazil

恩讐の
彼方に霞む
真珠湾

Pearl Harbor—
in the dimmed realm
beyond love and hate.

onshu no
kanata ni kasumu
shinju-wan

宮崎笛人
サンガブリエル

Fueto Miyazaki
San Gabriel, California

影絵にも
似て十二月
七日過ぐ

Like a shadow picture,
the day of December seventh
has passed by.

kagee nimo
nite juni gatsu
nanoka sugu

宮崎笛人
サンガブリエル

Fueto Miyazaki
San Gabriel, California

異人種の
るつぼさながら
アロハ祭

A crucible
of different races—
the Aloha Festival.

ijinshu no
rutsubo sanagara
aroha-matsuri

宮崎笛人
サンガブリエル

Fueto Miyazaki
San Gabriel, California

137

人皆を
レイに繋ぎて
椰子の春

Joining everyone
with flowering leis—
spring palm trees!

hito mina wo
rei ni tsunagite
yashi no haru.

森山弘子
ホノルル

Hiroko Moriyama
Honolulu, Hawai'i

アロハオエ
世界を跨ぐ
天の川

Aloha oe!
The milky way is crossing
over the world.

aroha oe
sekai wo matagu
ama no kawa

森山弘子
ホノルル

Hiroko Moriyama
Honolulu, Hawai'i

139

風薫る
氏の遺志生かす
研究所

A fragrant breeze
over the Peace Institute . . .
his legacy!

kaze kaoru
shi no ishi ikasu
kenkyusho

本永きよみ
ヒロ

Kiyomi Motonaga
Hilo, Hawai'i

国際の
祭りに触れし
手の温み

International Festival—
touching the warm hands
of everybody.

kokusai no
matsuri ni fureshi
te no nukumi

本永きよみ
ヒロ

Kiyomi Motonaga
Hilo, Hawai'i

太平洋
永久に架けたる
平和橋

Pacific Ocean—
it's a peace bridge
that spans eternally.

taiheiyo
towa ni kaketaru
heiwa-bashi

村田ヘンリー
サクラメント

Henry Murata
Sacramento, California

一世の
軌跡響くや
盆太鼓

Bon drum beats—
issei's legacy
sounding loudly.

issei no
kiseki hibiku ya
bon taiko

長岡明子
ホノルル

Akiko Nagaoka
Honolulu, Hawai'i

風薫る
誉れ尊し
二世隊

The nisei regiment marching
with distinguished honors . . .
a fragrant breeze blows.

kaze kaoru
homare totoshi
nisei-tai

長岡明子
ホノルル

Akiko Nagaoka
Honolulu, Hawai'i

合掌に
世界は一つ
弥陀の春

Joining our hands,
we are one world
in Amitabha's spring.

gassho ni
sekai wa hitotsu
mida no haru

中西美沙
ホノルル

Misa Nakanishi
Honolulu, Hawai'i

春爛漫
合わす両手が
和の世界

Spring in all its glory,
clasping both hands in prayer,
is the world of harmony.

haru ranman
awasu ryote ga
wa no sekai

中西美沙
ホノルル

Misa Nakanishi
Honolulu, Hawai'i

愛の枝
ひろごるカマニ
青葉かな

Verdant leaves
of kamani spreading
the branches of love.

ai no eda
hirogoru kamani
aoba kana

西村虹山
ヒロ

Kozan Nishimura
Hilo, Hawai'i

登り来る
人にゆずりぬ
滝の径

I yield to a man
coming up the lane
to the waterfall.

nobori kuru
hito ni yuzurin
taki no michi

西村虹山
ヒロ

Kozan Nishimura
Hilo, Hawai'i

夕焼けの
彼方に描く
浄土かな

The Pure Land is
painted far beyond
the sunset glow.

yuyake no
kanata ni egaku
jodo kana

野々村青風
サンフランシスコ

Seifu Nonomura
San Francisco, California

一湾に
街の灯あつめ
夕涼し

Gathering
the town lights in the bay—
cool evening breeze.

ichiwan ni
machi no hi atsume
yu suzushi

緒方光洋
ヒロ

Koyo Ogata
Hilo, Hawai'i

椰子涼し
白砂にしみる
波の音

Cool breeze in the palm trees—
the sounds of waves
seep into the white sands.

yashi suzushi
hakusa ni shimiru
nami no oto

緒方光洋
ヒロ

Koyo Ogata
Hilo, Hawai'i

空爆を
知らぬ子よ掌に
雪を受け

Children who do not know
about the air raid
catch snowflakes on their palms.

kubaku wo
shiranu ko yo teni
yuki wo uke

坂本こーじん
京都

Kohjin Sakamoto
Kyoto, Japan

パンチボールの
大樹に風の
光りけり

The leaves of a giant tree
in Punchbowl Cemetery
flicker in the breeze.

panchiboru no
taiju ni kaze no
hikari keri

篠原三枝
ヒロ

Mitsue Shinohara
Hilo, Hawai'i

四海を亘る
五月の空の
清しさよ

How refreshing is
the May sky,
embracing the four seas.

shikai wo wataru
satsuki no sora no
sugashisa yo

篠原三枝
ヒロ

Mitsue Shinohara
Hilo, Hawai'i

遥かなる
アリゾナ廟に
二重虹

Appearing far yonder
over the Arizona Memorial—
double rainbows!

harukanaru
arizona-byo ni
niju-niji

庄司光伯
ホノルル

Mitsuharu Shoji
Honolulu, Hawai'i

秋光や
先達（移民）の魂
いつまでも

Autumn sunbeams—
the souls of the ancestors
for eternity.

shuko ya
sendachi (imin) no tama
itsumademo

末岡菊江
ホノルル

Kikue Sueoka
Honolulu, Hawai'i

緑蔭に
手話の人坐し
峡の寺

At a temple in the valley
a man sits in the shade of trees,
talking with his hands.

ryokuin ni
shuwa no hito zashi
kai no tera

鈴木みつ
サンフランシスコ

Mitsu Suzuki
San Francisco, California

157

万緑や
今日も小鳥の
歌楽し

A myriad of green leaves—
birds singing merrily
today again!

banryoku ya
kyo mo kotori no
uta tanoshi

山下てい女
ホノルル

Teijo Yamashita
Honolulu, Hawai'i